# WEAPONS
## OF THE
# GULF
# WAR

# WEAPONS
## OF THE
# GULF WAR

S. L. Mayer

Charles Percival

Ian V. Hogg

Antony Preston

Crescent Books
New York

This 1991 edition published by Crescent Books, distributed by Outlet Book Company, Inc., a Random House Company, 225 Park Avenue South, New York, New York 10003.

Produced by
Brompton Books Corporation
15 Sherwood Place,
Greenwich, CT 06830

ISBN 0-517-06672-6

10 9 8 7 6 5 4 3 2 1

Printed and bound in Hong Kong

PAGE 1: A Patriot missile launcher stands at the ready as night falls over Saudi Arabia.

PAGES 2-3: A spectacular but ineffective anti-aircraft barrage lights up the night sky over Baghdad as the first Allied air attacks begin.

THIS PAGE, TOP: An RAF Tornado GR1 fighter bomber banks under full power in a training flight over Saudi Arabia.

THIS PAGE, CENTER: Iraqi artillery in action.

THIS PAGE, BOTTOM: The battleship USS *Wisconsin* at anchor in the Gulf during the Desert Shield prelude to the fighting.

# CONTENTS

# INTRODUCTION

## by S. L. Mayer

When the forces of Saddam Hussein's Iraq invaded Kuwait on 2 August, 1990, most of the nations of the world were shocked. They ought not to have been. Earlier in the year Iraq succeeded in ending the eight-year struggle against Iran, in the belief that the West, particularly the United States, would do nothing if Iraq turned her attentions toward oil-rich Kuwait instead, and that the neighbouring Arab States, such as Saudi Arabia, would do nothing in particular without the Americans. Iraq was right about the latter point and wrong about the former. The force of the American response as well as the response from the rest of the international community, particularly the Soviet Union, was as shocking to Saddam Hussein as the invasion was to the forces allied against him. Excluding any examination of the personal psyches of the American leadership, particularly that of President Bush, there are three principal reasons for the intensity of the American reaction and, hence, the support of its friends, neutrals and even its most recent enemies throughout the world:

1. Oil. If Kuwait's principal export were oranges, it is doubtful if the UN would have reacted as it did. With Kuwaiti oil a madman like Saddam Hussein would be in a strong position to take over the entire Gulf region, including Saudi Arabia, Bahrain and the United Arab Emirates. This would place him in charge of over 40 percent of the world's oil supplies, and make him the principal supplier of oil to Western Europe and Japan. Such a thing was not in the interests of the United States or its allies.

2. Nuclear capability. The nuclear reactor, supplied by France in 1976, had been blown up by the Israelis in a much-criticized air strike in June 1981. Since that time more had been built. It was thought that Iraq was close to being capable of launching a nuclear weapon of some sort.

3. Chemical warfare capability. Iraqi chemical weapons had been developed during the war with Iran. Combined with the missile power which Iraq had at its disposal, and in the hands of the fourth largest land army in the world, these weapons were a potential threat to every neighbouring state, particularly Saudi Arabia and Israel, and to any hostile armed force. The longer the United States waited for Iraqi power to grow, the more difficult it would be to dislodge Saddam Hussein from power. The Western powers had little choice but to stifle Iraq at once, using Kuwait as an excuse.

In every war since 1945, whether or not one of the two superpowers was directly involved, the conflict was a surrogate war pitting the weapons of the one superpower against the other. In more recent years the plots thickened when weapons of the various European states were pitted against one another, occasionally utilising the weapons of one or another of the two Great Powers. An example of this development was the Biafra War in Nigeria, which was, in effect, a surrogate war in weapons terms, between Britain and France, with the United States and Sweden being the secondary players throughout most of it. Likewise, the earlier stages of the Vietnam War pitted US weapons (and personnel later on) against the weapons of France and China (with some personnel earlier on), with the Soviet Union remaining in the wings until the second and third acts of the drama brought the Russians to center stage. The Gulf War of 1991 was also a war of surrogates. Although the United States, Britain, France and their NATO allies stood firmly against Iraq on the battlefield, in the war of weapons the picture was far less clear, as this book will show. In some ironic instances, Western allies were fighting the weapons which their own nationals had built

RIGHT: President Bush visits with some of the US troops in the Gulf on Thanksgiving Day 1990. During November 1990 it was announced that the size of the US force in the Gulf would be substantially increased.

LEFT: Iraqi leader Saddam Hussein at an Arab conference in 1990, before the Kuwait invasion.

ABOVE: Iraqi Foreign Minister Tariq Aziz answers newsmen's questions during his abortive January 9th meeting in Geneva with US Secretary of State James Baker.

and shipped to Iraq. Their own troops were placed in mortal danger by chemical, biological, nuclear and conventional weapons supplied by manufacturers in their home countries or in the countries of their closest political allies. This book, therefore, is about the facts behind the surrogate as well as the actual Gulf War.

Beginning this brief survey, let us look at nuclear power. The French supplied the first nuclear reactor which the Israelis destroyed. Two other reactors were built since, one by France and the other by the Soviet Union. Roughly 12.6 kg of highly enriched uranium originally supplied by France was still held by Iraq at the beginning of the conflict. German scientists have helped Saddam Hussein build the centrifuges needed for making a rudimentary nuclear weapon. Indeed, in 1989 Iraq bought from a British company the special magnets which are used to hold the centrifuges in place when they rotate at high speed. In that same year the United States Department of Commerce blocked an attempt by an American company to ship Iraq vacuum pumps used in enrichment plants. But what Iraq had was barely enough. At the start of the Gulf War they were manufacturing their own magnets and were thought to be only a few months away from being capable of launching primitive nuclear devices against nearby enemies.

In the field of chemical warfare America's allies were very helpful to Saddam Hussein. As early as 1975 Iraq approached an American company, Pfaudler, in Rochester, New York, to build a factory for making pesticides. Such factories can also be used for the manufacture of chemical weapons. When the company's representatives discovered that Iraq was interested in building a huge plant capable of handling 1200 tons of toxic materials annually, they became aware that pes-

ABOVE: The US military leaders for the war: General Colin Powell, Chairman of the Joint Chiefs of Staff, Defense Secretary Dick Cheney, and General Norman Schwarzkopf, US commander in the Gulf.

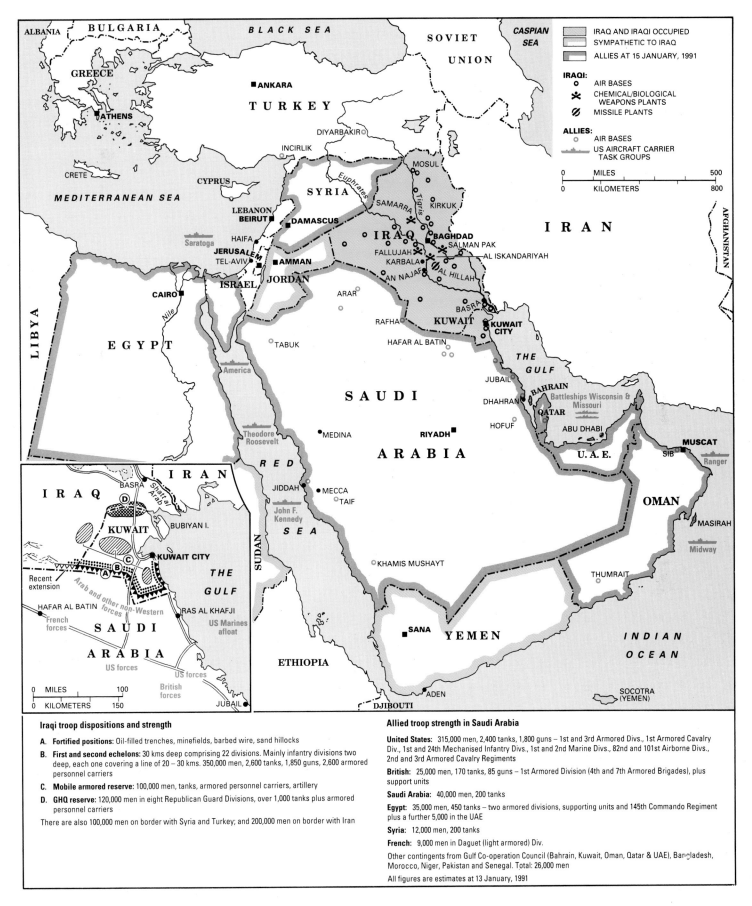

ABOVE: The situation on the eve of the coalition offensive.

**Iraqi troop dispositions and strength**

**A. Fortified positions:** Oil-filled trenches, minefields, barbed wire, sand hillocks

**B. First and second echelons:** 30 kms deep comprising 22 divisions. Mainly infantry divisions two deep, each one covering a line of 20 – 30 kms. 350,000 men, 2,600 tanks, 1,850 guns, 2,600 armored personnel carriers

**C. Mobile armored reserve:** 100,000 men, tanks, armored personnel carriers, artillery

**D. GHQ reserve:** 120,000 men in eight Republican Guard Divisions, over 1,000 tanks plus armored personnel carriers

There are also 100,000 men on border with Syria and Turkey; and 200,000 men on border with Iran

**Allied troop strength in Saudi Arabia**

**United States:** 315,000 men, 2,400 tanks, 1,800 guns – 1st and 3rd Armored Divs., 1st Armored Cavalry Div., 1st and 24th Mechanised Infantry Divs., 1st and 2nd Marine Divs., 82nd and 101st Airborne Divs., 2nd and 3rd Armored Cavalry Regiments

**British:** 25,000 men, 170 tanks, 85 guns – 1st Armored Division (4th and 7th Armored Brigades), plus support units

**Saudi Arabia:** 40,000 men, 200 tanks

**Egypt:** 35,000 men, 450 tanks – two armored divisions, supporting units and 145th Commando Regiment plus a further 5,000 in the UAE

**Syria:** 12,000 men, 200 tanks

**French:** 9,000 men in Daguet (light armored) Div.

Other contingents from Gulf Co-operation Council (Bahrain, Kuwait, Oman, Qatar & UAE), Bangladesh, Morocco, Niger, Pakistan and Senegal. Total: 26,000 men

All figures are estimates at 13 January, 1991

LEFT: Protestors during a pro-Iraqi rally in Amman, Jordan, in January 1991, shortly before the Allied air offensive began.

ticides were not the purpose of such a large facility. Then Iraq approached Britain's ICI, and the proposal was equally rejected. But other companies on the continent of Europe were more helpful, notably Germany's Fritz Werner, who helped engineer the deal which sent $11 million worth of heavy duty pumps and chemicals, including trichloride, used in the manufacture of nerve gas, to Iraq. Subsequently, Iraq bought large quantities of chemicals such as thiodiglycol in Europe and the United States. This can be used for printing and photographic developing, but it can also be used as a key component in the manu-

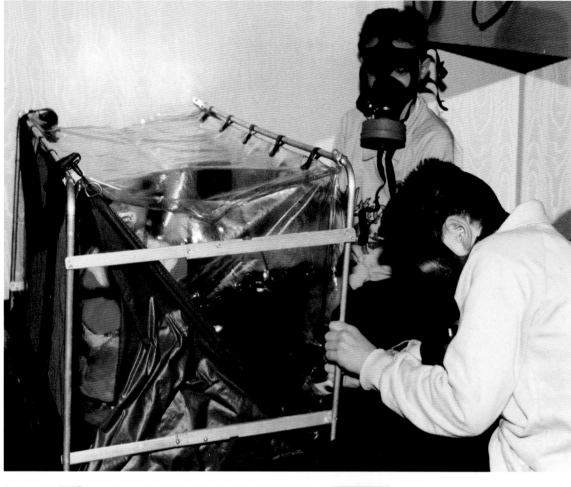

LEFT: Anti-gas precautions for an Israeli child in the face of Saddam's threat of missile and chemical weapons attack.

BELOW: Rescue personnel sift through the debris after an Iraqi Scud missile hit buildings in the Israeli city of Tel Aviv. Saddam hoped that his attacks on Israel would provoke a direct military response and split the coalition against him.

RIGHT: One of the first indications of Saddam's dangerous militarism noted by many in the West arose from the so-called 'Supergun' affair. Here parts of this supposed giant long-range weapon are held by Greek customs officers en route to Iraq after being ordered under a pretext from a British manufacturer, April 1990.

ABOVE: The remains of a Patriot missile go on public display in Dhahran, Saudi Arabia, after it had successfully intercepted an incoming Scud missile.

facture of mustard gas. In 1983 Phillips Petroleum shipped 500 tons of thiodiglycol to Iraq from Belgium but became suspicious when 500 tons was reordered. The second shipment did not go forward, but by this time Iraq was making its own mustard gas and using it in the war against Iran. Biological weapons, such as those disseminating anthrax, were also developed by German and other Continental companies.

As the authors of this book will show, many of the missiles, ships, guns and planes, as well as the rockets used on them, were supplied by the Soviet Union, Iraq's erstwhile ally and the West's erstwhile, traditional foe. However, many others were developed in Western countries. France provided many types of aircraft. Germany helped develop Iraq's missile capability. German technicians helped to modify the Scud missiles so as to

bring Israel within range. Germany provided technology to help Iraq build its chemical arsenal. Belgium provided various types of small arms, for which that small country is justly famous, while for a time denying the British army spare ammunition for the same weapons. Germany was slow to provide spare parts for the British Tornados in the first weeks of the war while German companies continued to supply their Iraqi clients, not with Tornado parts, to be sure, but with components for the weapons destroyed during the heavy bombing by the UN forces.

It is difficult to recall the heady days of 1989 in which Helmut Kohl was hailed as the saviour of Germany and the arbiter of European unity. British politicians, such as Nicholas Ridley and Prime Minister Margaret Thatcher, were brought down, in part for their reluctance to support enthusiastically the cause of swift European unity, a Europe which, perforce, would be led by a recently unified Germany. It has often been stated that war is the apotheosis of nationalism. A national state amasses its military force, its people, its youth, its combined energies, to defeat the foreign foe. Criticism is muffled if not silenced. In an alliance, such as NATO, all the powers within it are supposed to act in concert, particularly when one of its member states, Turkey, is threatened, as was the case in the early stages of the Gulf War. But what was the result? Britain and the United States, supported by nations of the Commonwealth and other friendly nations such as the Netherlands, Italy, France and Spain, sent either ships or troops or both, in the case of France, to the Gulf. Behind the scenes, France worked for a peaceful solution to the crisis up to the eleventh hour prior to 15 January 1991 and beyond, while Germany continued to pretend, like Japan, that it could not and would not act with the UN and its NATO allies, while, behind the scenes, expertise and weapons trickled on into Iraq. Europe made no unified stance during the Gulf War. Indeed, three Europes emerged: one, led by Britain, supported the United States and the United Nations wholeheartedly; a second, supported both sides to a greater or lesser extent, and topping this list were France, Germany and Belgium; the third Europe sat on the sidelines, adopting a wait-and-see policy. Among those nations were Denmark and other Scandinavian states. One casualty of the Gulf War surely will be the speed and progress of European unity. Once again, as in so many other conflicts of the 20th century, Britain and the United States led the fight against the aggressor state, led by a lunatic. The origin and nature of the Weapons of the Gulf War are a symbol of this fact.

# AIRCRAFT and AIR WEAPONS

## THE OPPOSING FORCES

Secrecy and surprise are an important part of wars, and the Gulf War has been no exception. Even in its brief course, unexpected weapons were used, and both sides issued 'disinformation' on their strengths and weaknesses. Any estimate on equipment and numbers at this stage can only be provisional.

Well over one thousand combat aircraft and helicopters were deployed in the Gulf by the coalition forces, most of them belonging to the United States. Current American doctrine is that if war is necessary, overwhelming force should be used to bring it to an end as swiftly as possible. Aircraft were present from the US Air Force, Army, Marines and Air National Guard, together with at least six US Navy aircraft carriers.

After the Americans, the largest air contingents were provided by Great Britain and Saudi Arabia, each with about 200 aircraft and helicopters. France, Italy, Canada, Qatar and the Royal Kuwaiti Air Force (RKAF) all provided smaller forces. Syria and Egypt, although they have sizeable air forces, sent only ground troops. Turkey, which is a member of NATO, was used as a base for US Air

PREVIOUS PAGE: A USAF F-117A 'stealth' aircraft of the 37th Tactical Fighter Wing refuels in flight from a KC-10A Extender high over the Saudi Arabian desert.

LEFT: F/A-18 Hornets of US Navy Squadron VFA-25 'Fist of the Fleet' in the Gulf.

RIGHT: A USAF B-52G of 2nd Bomber Wing, based at RAF Fairford in Great Britain. By refueling in flight these aircraft flew long-range bombing missions over iraq and Kuwait during the war.

BELOW: An A-4KU Skyhawk of the Royal Kuwaiti Air Force with the 'Free Kuwait' markings added to aircraft that escaped the Iraqi occupation and later flew against Iraq.

LEFT: Panavia Tornado GR1 strike aircraft from one of four Royal Air Force Squadrons deployed in the Gulf.

Force raids into Iraq. Aircraft and missile batteries from a number of NATO countries, including Germany and the Netherlands, were supplied for Turkey's defense.

Members of the coalition have many aircraft and helicopters in common, mostly of the latest types, and their pilots are very highly trained, but few had previous combat experience. All aircraft were integrated into the same command structure, so that different nationalities could operate together without problems.

The Iraqi air forces were organised and equipped along Soviet lines, with a separate Air Defense Command. Altogether, the Iraqi Air Force, or *Al Quwwat al Jawwiya al*

*Iraqiya*, had roughly 150 modern fighters and bombers, 350 older aircraft, and 200 helicopters at the beginning of the war. On paper, Iraqi air power looked strong enough to give the coalition some problems. However, numerous modifications were carried out to Iraqi equipment during the Iran-Iraq War, and it was not clear how many of the Iraqi aircraft could still fly even at the outset. Iraqi pilots were judged to be greatly inferior to most of their opponents.

## DOCTRINE AND STRATEGY

While high commands take considerable care not to give away their plans, it is possible to make an informed assessment of the kind of war that both sides were trying to fight.

The basic coalition strategy was to use high-technology precision air strikes to knock out Iraq's communications and supply systems, and then massive bombardment against Iraqi troops, leaving them leaderless and weak before the land battle started. With the Iraqi Air Force out of the way, the full weight of air power could be used to help the land forces. The coalition members were anxious to hold their own casualties to an absolute minimum, and some airmen hoped that air power alone might force an Iraqi surrender without the need for a land battle.

ABOVE: A Soviet-made SS-1 Scud-B missile ready to fire on its mobile launcher. The Scud needs to be fueled in this position with its launcher stationary for up to an hour before firing.

Iraqi strategy seems to have been based on outlasting its vastly superior opponents, until the level of their own casualties or political opinion at home forced them to give in. In order to create political pressure on the Arab members of the coalition, Iraq hoped to draw Israel into the war against it by missile and air attacks. It was hoped that extensive underground bunkers would protect Iraqi command centers, supplies, troops and even aircraft from all but the largest bombs. Rather than being drawn into an air battle the Iraqi Air Force was held back as a constant small threat, making it difficult for the coalition members to switch their aircraft to the land battle, or make major helicopter movements. After about a week the United States introduced the laser-guided 5000-

RIGHT: Radar plotters of the Royal Saudi Air Force and a US advisor on board a Saudi E-3A Sentry AWACS.

ABOVE: An E-8A J-STARS, used jointly by the USAF and the US Army to co-ordinate battle in the air and on the ground with its downward-looking radar.

pound 'bunker buster' bomb, capable of penetrating hardened Iraqi aircraft shelters. Iraq then flew about 150 of its aircraft for safety to Iran, where they remained throughout the war. About 20 Iraqi aircraft were captured still inside their shelters during the ground war.

## COMMAND AND EARLY WARNING AIRCRAFT

Modern air combat is a matter of interpreting the battlefield and switching aircraft rapidly from target to target. Although they got little publicity, the airborne command posts were the most important aircraft in the war.

The USAF E-8A J-STARS (Joint Surveillance and Target Attack Radar System), converted Boeing 707 airliners of which at least two were in the Gulf, can detect enemy tanks moving over one hundred miles away. They

fly, protected by fighters, high above the battlefield, picking up targets and directing aircraft onto them. Assistance comes from the E-3A/B Sentry AWACS (Airborne Early Warning And Control Systems), another converted Boeing 707 flown by the USAF and Royal Saudi Air Force (RSAF), which controls friendly aircraft and detects enemy air movement. The US Navy used the Grumman E-2C Hawkeye, a smaller carrier-based version of the AWACS. On the first night of the war these aircraft coordinated over 400 Allied aircraft and 100 missiles onto at least 200 different targets in Iraq and Kuwait within 45 minutes, without loss.

Electronically, the Iraqis were vastly inferior to the coalition members. Iraq could supplement its ground radars with one or two Adnan-1 AEW aircraft, a locally modified version of the Soviet-built Ilyushin Il-76MD Mainstay (NATO reporting name), which is broadly comparable to the E-3 Sentry.

## MISSILES

The Gulf War has shown how difficult it is for even the strongest air force to defend against unmanned missiles. The Iraqi missile campaign was, however, far less effective than that of the Americans.

On the Allied side this conflict saw the first use in war of the General Dynamics AGM/BGM-109 Tomahawk cruise missile, which is fired vertically, but then flies up to 800 miles at sub-sonic speeds a few feet off the ground by following a satellite-generated 'map' of its route, arriving within 100 feet of its target. The Tomahawk can carry a nuclear bomb, but those used in the Gulf had 900-pound conventional warheads. The two US Navy versions, known as the Tomahawk Land Attack Missile or TLAM/C and D, have been fired from battleships, cruisers, destroyers and the torpedo tubes of attack submarines. Tomahawks can also be launched from USAF B-1 and B-52 bombers and from mobile ground launchers, although there have been no reports of this happening in the Gulf.

For defense against tactical ballistic missiles the United States has the Raytheon MIM-104 Patriot antiaircraft missile system, which can also intercept incoming missiles in the last few seconds of their fall to earth. For defense against air attack the coalition members deployed several SAM systems, including the Raytheon MIM-23B Improved Hawk, the British Aerospace Rapier, and the Euromissile Roland, made by France and Germany, which has also been sold to Iraq.

The principal Iraqi offensive weapon in the war was the Soviet made SS-1 Scud-B ballistic missile, for which Iraq had about 30 fixed and 35 mobile launchers. The Scud-B is an elderly and inaccurate weapon, carrying a 2000-pound warhead about 170 miles. It can be fitted with a nuclear or chemical warhead, but before the war Iraq was not believed to have this capability. The Iraqis have developed two longer-range versions, the Hussein with a 1000-pound warhead and a range of 400 miles, and the Abbas with a 400-pound warhead and a range of over 500 miles, enough to reach Israel. These missiles take about an hour to prepare for firing, and have a flight time of less than eight minutes to target. Before the war Iraq was developing, together with other countries, the Condor-2 precision-guided ballistic missile with a longer range than the Abbas, but this is not believed to have been in service. Iraq claims on one occasion to have fired a salvo of three Hijara missiles, a previously unknown type,

RIGHT: A MIM-104 Patriot Missile, which carries a 200-pound warhead, at the moment of firing.

LEFT: A Paveway laser-guided bomb carried beneath the wing of a USAF F-16 Fighting Falcon. The Paveway head locks on to a laser beam illuminating the target and steers the bomb with moveable fins down to the point of impact.

LEFT: A Martin Marietta 2000-pound Walleye glide bomb, steered to the target by a television camera in its nose.

RIGHT: An AGM-84E SLAM missile being launched from a US Navy F/A-18 Hornet.

LEFT: A Patriot launcher, equipped with four missiles. In the background is a USAF F-15C Eagle of 1st Tactical Fighter Wing.,

BELOW: The MPQ-53 radar for a battery of eight Patriot launchers. This can control up to five Patriot missiles at once, intercepting Scuds as they fall to earth at speeds of Mach 8 or more.

at Israel. There were also reports of Iraq possessing the Soviet-made SS-12 Scaleboard precision-guided ballistic missile.

For air defense, Iraq relied principally on over 400 Soviet-made SAM launchers, some of them the latest SA-8 Gecko and SA-13 Gopher, which are far less susceptible to infra-red or chaff decoys than older types. Iraq had no antimissile systems, but did shoot down cruise missiles with antiaircraft fire and even claimed to have fired them back at their owners.

Although not officially admitted, Israel is widely known to have nuclear weapons as well as a precision-guided ballistic missile, the Jericho-2, with sufficient range to reach Baghdad. In 1990 Israel tested its own antimissile system, but this ran into technical problems. A month before the war the United States supplied Israel with the P1 version of the Patriot, followed by the P2 version with American crews after the first Abbas attacks.

## ELECTRONIC WARFARE AIRCRAFT

In response to SAM defenses, most air forces have specialist Electronic Warfare (EW) aircraft to support their combat missions by jamming and attacking enemy radars.

The main Allied EW aircraft were the USAF General Dynamics EF-111 Raven (nicknamed the 'Spark Vark') and the Grumman EA-6B Prowler, used by the US Navy and Marines. The USAF also has a number of EC-130E/H Hercules transports converted for EW, and the AC-130H Hercules 'Pave Spectre' gunship, which detects small enemy ground targets such as missile sites and brings an extremely heavy concentration of fire onto them. The famous McDonnell-Douglas F-4 Phantom II made probably its last appearance in war for the USAF in two 'Wild Weasel' F-4G squadrons, equipped with the AGM-88A HARM (High speed Anti-Radiation Missile), which homes onto the signals put out by aircraft detection radar. Making its first appearance was the RAF equivalent,

the ALARM (Air-Launched Anti-Radiation Missile), carried on the Panavia Tornado F3 IDS. Virtually all bombers and ground attack aircraft also carry ECM (Electronic Counter Measures) pods for limited self-defense.

The Iraqi Air Force is not known to have had any specialist EW or radar suppression aircraft or missiles.

## RECONNAISSANCE AIRCRAFT

The Allied air strategy in particular depended on good information about the effects of their own attacks, for which sophisticated reconnaissance aircraft were vital.

For deep reconnaissance over Iraq the USAF used the Lockheed TR-1A long-range high-altitude reconnaissance aircraft, based outside the Gulf. For tactical reconnaissance modified versions of other aircraft were used, including the Lockheed F-117A 'stealth' aircraft, the RAF's Panavia Tornado GR1R and the French Mirage F1CR. For artillery observation the US Army and Marines still use the elderly Rockwell OV-10 Bronco piston-engined light spotter plane. To assist naval forces in the Gulf, the RAF sent a few land-based British Aerospace Nimrod MR1 long-range maritime reconnaissance aircraft.

Iraq is believed to have adapted a squadron of its Soviet-made MiG-25A Foxbat high-

speed, high-altitude interceptor aircraft to the reconnaissance role as the MiG-25R. These are easier to detect than the latest reconnaissance aircraft, but rely on outpacing their opponents at high altitude.

## AIR SUPERIORITY FIGHTERS

This war was the first major test of a new generation of 'agile' air superiority fighters, capable of outmaneuvering other aircraft and even missiles at high speed.

The principal Allied air superiority fighter was the single-seat McDonnell-Douglas F-15C Eagle, flown by the USAF and RSAF.

ABOVE: A USAF F-111F 'Aardvark' of 493rd Tactical Fighter Squadron, 48th Tactical Fighter Wing, passing in front of an EF-111 Raven of 388th Electronic Countermeasures Squadron.

LEFT: A Mirage F1EQ firing an Exocet anti-shipping missile. One such attack was attempted by the Iraqis during the war but the Mirage was shot down by US carrier aircraft.

ABOVE: A Buccaneer S2B of 12 Squadron RAF in its hardened shelter at Bahrain airbase.

The F-15C normally carries AIM-9G Sidewinder and AIM-7F Sparrow missiles. The second half of the war saw the first deployment on the F-15C of the long-awaited AIM-120 AMRAAM (Advanced Medium Range Anti-Aircraft Missile), a 'fire-and-forget' missile with a range of about 40 miles, but it was never fired in anger. With only light opposition from the Iraqi Air Force the other main USAF agile fighter, the General Dynamics F-16 Fighting Falcon, was used largely as a ground attack aircraft. The

US Navy's swing-wing Grumman F-14 Tomcat, biggest and heaviest of the agile fighters, carries Sidewinders and the AIM-54C Phoenix, which also has a 'fire and forget' capability. Fighter cover for French missions came from their Mirage 2000E fighter with Super Matra R530 and R550 Magic missiles, in use for the first time. The RAF used the Panavia Tornado F3, carrying the Sidewinder and the British-built Sky Flash. Although not an agile fighter, this interceptor version of the Tornado was capable of outflying all Iraqi aircraft except the MiG-29.

The biggest threat to Allied aircraft came from about 20 of the latest Soviet-built MiG-29 Fulcrum fighters, the only agile fighter Iraq possesses, equipped with AA-9 and AA-10 'fire and forget' missiles, a 'look down, shoot down' radar and an infra-red

ABOVE: Cutaway drawing of a McDonnell-Douglas F/A-18 Hornet of the US Navy. This example is shown with Sidewinder and Sparrow missiles and Walleye bombs.

targeting system for close range. Since both the Germans and the Syrians also fly the Fulcrum it should have presented few surprises, but by reputation it is currently the most maneuverable fighter in service. In addition, Iraq had about 50 of the swing-wing MiG-23MS Flogger interceptor (Flogger-B, Flogger-E and Flogger-H variants), together with perhaps 20 MiG-25A Foxbats. These are updated versions of fighters from an earlier generation, and would have given most Allied aircraft at least some trouble. The remainder of Iraq's fighters, about 200 aircraft, were types that were of some value against Iran but are obsolete in modern war, chiefly the MiG-21 Fishbed, its Chinese equivalent the Xian F-7, and the even older Chinese Shenyang F-6.

bomb. The most unusual type in service is the McDonnell-Douglas/British Aerospace AV-8B Harrier II 'jump jet' with vertical takeoff and landing capability, flown by the US Marines. The Harrier's ability to manage with a very short runway, or none at all, makes it ideal for supporting amphibious operations. Making its first appearance in war was the USAF McDonnell-Douglas F-15E Strike Eagle, the two-seat multirole version of the F-15 Eagle.

The British and French ground attack squadrons in the Gulf flew the Sepecat Jaguar GR1 and Jaguar A respectively. This is a single-seat supersonic aircraft which can carry up to eight 1000-pound bombs. Qatar and Kuwait fly the French-built Mirage F1 as a ground attack aircraft, and Kuwait also

## GROUND ATTACK FIGHTERS

Most modern fighters can perform a double role as light bombers or ground attack aircraft. These can be counted as fighters or bombers depending on the weapons fit for the mission.

Most versatile of the ground attack fighters is the McDonnell Douglas F/A-18 Hornet, flown in the Gulf by the US Navy and Marines, and the Royal Canadian Air Force as the CF-18A. The dual F/A designation means that the Hornet is officially both a fighter and an attack aircraft. It normally carries Sidewinders, but can take the AMRAAM or the Paveway laser-guided

flies a few elderly American-built Douglas A-4KU Skyhawks.

The Iraqis had about 90 of the modern French-built Dassault-Breguet Mirage F1EQ, which can also carry the Exocet anti-shipping missile or the Soviet AS-14 Kedge air-to-surface missile. Some of Iraq's 80 MiG-27 Flogger-Fs, the ground attack version of the Flogger which flew in the Iran-Iraq War, were also still in service. The rest of Iraq's ground attack aircraft were Soviet types obsolete in modern war, such as the Sukhoi Su-22 Fitter-J, the Su-20 Fitter-C, and even the original Su-7 Fitter. Virtually all of Iraq's ground attack aircraft could have been used to deliver chemical or biological weapons.

ABOVE: Two RAF Jaguar GR1s (nearest the camera) and a Tornado GR1 on routine patrol over Saudi Arabia, all in the very muted camouflage scheme used by British aircraft in the Gulf.

ABOVE: A Panavia Tornado ADV (Air Defense Variant) of the Royal Saudi Air Force carrying four AIM-9G Sidewinders and four Sky Flash missiles.

RIGHT: Royal Saudi Air Force ground crew replace one of the two engines of a Saudi F-15C Eagle.

## CLOSE SUPPORT FIGHTERS

This type of specialist 'tank buster' aircraft is meant to support the ground battle by destroying enemy armor. It covers a gap in the speed and effectiveness range between high-performance aircraft and attack helicopters.

The USAF and US Marines both operated the Fairchild Republic A-10 Thunderbolt II, more usually known as the 'Warthog'. Designed to fly low and slow over the battlefield, the A-10 mounts a powerful 30mm antitank cannon, and can carry bombs or AGM-65 Maverick air-to-surface missiles. None of the other coalition members fly these specialist aircraft.

The Iraqi Air Force had about 30 of the Soviet equivalent to the A-10, the Sukhoi Su-25 Frogfoot, which is slightly different in appearance, but performs the same function and has much the same ability to fly low and slow. The Su-25 can also be used to deliver chemical weapons.

## BOMBERS

Precision bombing deep behind enemy lines was fundamental to Allied strategy. It was also the only effective means by which Iraq might have struck back against its enemies.

Attracting the greatest interest through its precision bombing ability, using the Paveway laser-guided bomb, was the USAF Lockheed F-117A 'stealth' aircraft, officially described as a fighter. Details are still highly secret, but the F-117A is claimed to be virtually invisible to radar and hard to detect on infra-red. The far larger Lockheed B-2 'stealth bomber' has, like the Rockwell B-1 bomber, not been reported in action in the Gulf. USAF bombing of military targets has instead been carried out by the venerable Boeing B-52G, which can carry up to fifty-one Mark 82 500-pound bombs, eighteen Mark 84 2000-pound bombs, or the equivalent in missiles. The F-15E has also been used in a deep strike bombing role, together with the ageing General Dynamics F-111F (also officially a fighter), nicknamed the 'Aardvark'. F-111Fs carrying 2000-pound Walleye television-guided glide-bombs have hit Iraqi targets with almost unbelievable accuracy.

The US Navy's principal carrier-based bomber is the Grumman A-6E Intruder, which can carry the AGM-84 Harpoon anti-shipping missile. This war has also seen the first use by an A-6E of the AGM-84E SLAM (Standoff Land Attack Missile) variant of the Harpoon, for attacking ground targets. The SLAM is guided to its target by a separate aircraft, in this case the US Navy's elderly Vought A-7E Corsair II carrier-based attack aircraft, which has largely been superceded by the F/A-18 Hornet.

The British, Saudis and Italians have all been flying the ground attack variant of the Panavia Tornado, known to the RAF as the GR1 variant, as a deep penetration bomber. All Tornados carry up to eight 1000-pound bombs. As an alternative, the RAF and Saudi Tornados have used the Hunting JP233 Low Altitude Airfield Attack System, which spreads a carpet of bomblets and mines along an enemy runway, while the Italian Tornados have a similar system made in Germany, the Raketen Technik MW-1. To assist the Tornados in precision bombing from medium altitudes the RAF flew out a squadron of

ABOVE: Captain Jim Glasgow with his A-10 'Warthog' of 23rd Tactical Fighter Wing USAF, normally based in Europe but in service in the Gulf, showing the Wing's famous 'Flying Tiger' nose insignia.

LEFT: For night bombing most coalition aircraft used infra-red video cameras to check on their own accuracy. Here an F-117A of 37th Tactical Fighter Wing has placed the crosshairs of its laser designator over the doors of an Iraqi hanger containing Scud missiles, which seconds later will be hit by its two Paveway bombs.

BELOW: Two A-7E Corsair IIs of Light Attack Squadron 72 US Navy, part of Carrier Air Wing 3 flying off the USS *John F. Kennedy* during operations in the Gulf.

LEFT: In darkness and silence an F-117A 'Stealth' refuels from a KC-135 Stratotanker before proceeding with its mission.

BELOW: An F-117A 'stealth' fighter of 37th Tactical Fighter Wing USAF.

Hawker Siddeley Buccaneer S2B bombers, equipped with Pave Spike laser designators, shortly after the start of the war.

The Iraqi Air Force had about 20 obsolete medium bombers, comprising Soviet-built Tupolev Tu-22 Blinders and Tu-16 Badgers with their Chinese copy, the Xian H-6D, which could have been used in an anti-shipping role. Intended to replace these were an equal number of Soviet-built Sukhoi Su-24MK Fencers, a swing-wing precision bomber broadly equivalent to the F-111 in performance. The Fencer is capable of carrying standoff missiles such as the AS-14 Kedge and of delivering chemical weapons.

## TRANSPORT AND IN-FLIGHT REFUELING AIRCRAFT

These are the aircraft that make everything else possible. About half of the sorties flown by coalition aircraft were either fighter operations or transport, refueling and support rather than strike missions.

The biggest of the coalition transports is the giant USAF Lockheed C-5 Galaxy, which was used to fly troops, stores and equipment into the Gulf, including the emergency supply of Patriot missiles to Israel. The USAF also flies the Lockheed C-141 Starlifter jet transport and the famous Lockheed C-130 Hercules, which is also flown by the RAF, RSAF, and the United Arab Emirates. Some of the RAF Hercules are the C-130H-30 C Mark 3 'stretched' version.

For in-flight refueling the USAF relies on the McDonnell-Douglas KC-10A Extender and the Boeing KC-135A Stratotanker. The F-117A 'stealth' is reported as able to refuel from these aircraft at night, without lights, and without breaking radio silence. The US Navy flies a tanker version of the A-6E Intruder designated as the KA-6D, and the US Marines a tanker version of the Hercules, the KC-130, also flown by the RSAF. The RAF had three types of tanker in the Gulf, the VC-10 and the Tristar, both modifications of civilian airliners, and the Victor K2.

The Iraqi Air Force had some 70 Soviet-

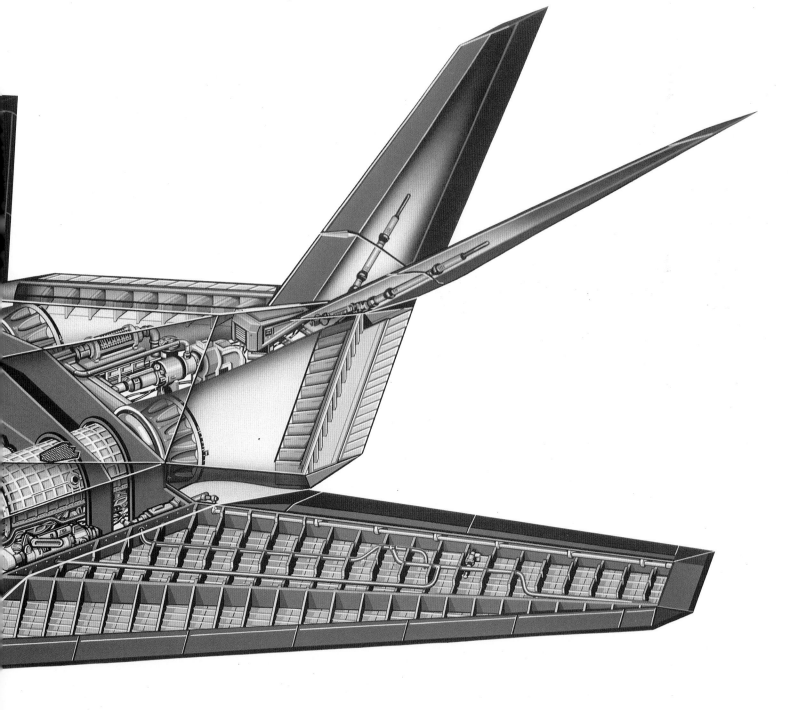

ABOVE: A VC-10 tanker aircraft of 101 Squadron RAF in the Gulf.

LEFT: A KC-135 Stratotanker refuels F-4G 'Wild Weasel' Phantom IIs of 52nd Tactical Fighter Wing USAF.

LEFT: A Chinook HC Mark 1 heavy lift helicopter from one of two RAF squadrons used in support of British Army operations.

BELOW: An Aerospatiale SA330 Puma HC1 of the RAF shows the problems for helicopters flying in desert conditions.

built transport aircraft, ranging from the elderly Antonov An-12 Cub to the modern Ilyushin Il-76 Candid jet. At least one of the Candid aircraft had been modified as an in-flight tanker.

## TRANSPORT HELICOPTERS

For the Allies the main battlefield transport helicopter was the US Army's Sikorsky UH-60 Black Hawk, which can carry a squad of 11 fully equipped infantrymen directly into combat. The US Navy flies the SH-60B SeaHawk version, and in 1990 Saudi Arabia took delivery of the VH-60 Desert Hawk, intended for Gulf conditions. In addition, the US Army and RAF both employed the Boeing Vertol CH-47 Chinook, and the British and French also used the Aerospatiale/Westland SA330 Puma. The US Marines can use the big Sikorsky CH-53E Super Stallion, holding up to forty combat troops, for their amphibious assaults, together with the Bell UH-1D Iroquois, better known as the 'Huey'.

The standard Iraqi battlefield transport helicopter was the Soviet-built Mil Mi-8 Hip, which carries about thirty troops. In addition Iraq had the Aerospatiale SA321 Super Frelon and SA330 Puma, which could both be used for anti-shipping strikes as well as transport.

ABOVE: Sikorsky VH-60 Desert Hawks of the Saudi Army, specially modified to cope with desert flying.

LEFT: The standard UH-60 Black Hawk flown by the US Army's 101st Air Assault Division in the war.

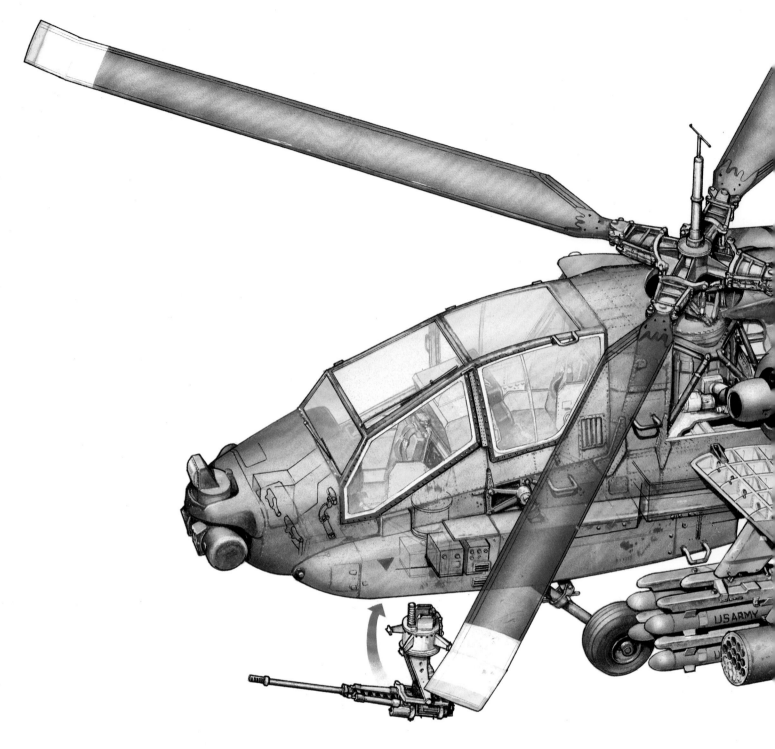

## ATTACK HELICOPTERS

This has been the first appearance in war of the US Army's McDonnell-Douglas AH-64 Apache, a sophisticated attack helicopter carrying the AGM-114A Hellfire antitank missile. The US Marines have used the Bell AH-1J Sea Cobra, a development from the HueyCobra of Vietnam fame, carrying either the AGM-71C TOW (Tube-launched, Optically-tracked, Wire-guided) missile or the Hellfire for close support. The British and French have both employed the Aerospatiale

SA341 Gazelle, and the British Army also sent the Westland Lynx, equipped with TOW. The Royal Navy Lynx successfully used the Sea Skua anti-shipping missile.

One of the most threatening Iraqi weapons was the Soviet-built Mil Mi-24 Hind, of which up to 40 may still have been flying at the out break of war. This very large attack helicopter can also carry a squad of infantry, and is generally regarded as the most capable helicopter gunship in the world. Iraq also had the Aerospatiale Gazelle, the German-built MBB BO-105, and the reliable McDonnell-Douglas 500M-D Defender.

ABOVE: The AH-64
Apache, the world's
most advanced and
sophisticated attack
helicopter, flown by 101st
Air Assault Division US
Army.

RIGHT: Soldiers of 101st
Air Assault Division
fitting an AH-64 Apache
with AGM-114A
missiles prior to takeoff.

# LAND WEAPONS

## ARMOR

The armored line-up in the Gulf presented a very interesting mixture of tried and untried designs, and many specialists will be examining the results of such armored combat as there was with particular interest.

The Iraqi army began the war with some 5500 main battle tanks of various types, almost all of Soviet origin. These included 1500 T54 and T55, 1500 T59 and T69, 1500 T62, 1000 T72, plus a handful of aged Chieftain, M47 and M60 tanks acquired years ago from Britain and the USA. All the Soviet tanks have been well tested in the eight-year war with Iran, and while they may not be at the forefront of technology, they have the virtue of being relatively simple vehicles to operate.

The US Army is equipped with the Abrams M1A1 main battle tank; this is far ahead of any Iraqi tank so far as technology goes, but it had never previously been tested in battle and was thus an unknown quantity. However, bearing in mind that the Abrams was designed to counter the best that the Soviet Union was likely to field during the present century, it seems fairly certain that it would have proved more than a match for anything

the Iraqi force might have put forward should they have better survived the Allied air attacks.

The Abrams is equipped with a powerful 120mm gun derived from a German design. A smooth-bore, it fires fin-stabilised armor-piercing ammunition comprising a depleted uranium penetrator carried in a light alloy 'sabot'. The sabot fits tightly in the bore but is discarded as soon as the shot leaves the muzzle, so that only the long, thin, highly-streamlined penetrator section flies to the target. Depleted uranium has absolutely no radio-active property; it is simply one of the heaviest and most dense metals in existence, and the impact of the thin but heavy dart at extremely high velocity simply punches through armor as if it were wood. Once inside, the penetrator is destabilised by the impact and ricochets around inside the tank destroying the mechanism and crew.

Alternatively a high explosive shaped charge projectile is available; this uses a specially-formed explosive charge to blast a hole through the armor, the flame and blast passing inside the target to cause maximum damage.

The British have fielded their Challenger tank, another design untested in war but, like the Abrams, developed with European

LEFT: A Syrian armored unit of 2500 men, with 100 Soviet T-62 tanks, arrives in Saudi Arabia by sea transport.

PREVIOUS PAGE: M1A1 Abrams tanks of the 24th US Infantry Division patrolling the Saudi Arabian desert.

LEFT: A British Army Challenger I main battle tank of the 7th Armoured Brigade maneuvers in the desert during exercises in October 1990.

BELOW: A US Army M551 Sheridan light tank, used for fast armored reconnaissance, with, in the background, a 'Hummer' utility vehicle armed with the TOW anti-armor missile.

ABOVE: Another view of the M551 Sheridan. The main armament is a short 6-inch gun capable of firing a powerful shaped charge anti-armor shell.

RIGHT: Cutaway view of the M1 Abrams tank, showing ammunition storage in the turret bustle, mechanical details, and the turret crowded with electronic fire control instrumentation.

conflict in mind and therefore full of the most modern technical equipment. It also has a 120mm gun, but this one is rifled, due to a British policy which maintains that a rifled gun is more versatile in the ammunition it fires. This seems to be borne out by experience, and the British gun fires a similar armor-piercing sabot round to the American, another sabot round which is spin-stabilised, plus a 'squash-head' shell, which is a British speciality. This is a thin-skinned shell filled with plastic explosive which is fired against armor. On striking, the shell peels away and

LEFT: A French-built AMX-30S main battle tank of the Saudi Arabian army in a hull-down position in the forward defensive line. The main armament is a 105mm gun, and alongside it is a 20mm automatic cannon.

RIGHT: M60A3 tanks of the Saudi Arabian army in a forward position, close to the Kuwait border. Saudi Arabia has over 250 of these tanks, armed with 105mm guns.

BELOW: Quatari troops pray to Mecca alongside an AMX-30S of the Quatar Army. The -30S version is specially modified for operation in deserts, with sand shields, special filters and a lower gear ratio.

deposits the plastic explosive tightly on the tank armor, then detonates it. The shock wave which is generated by the detonation passes into the armor, vibrates it, and detaches a heavy slab of metal from the inner face, which whirls around inside the tank and completely wrecks the interior.

No weapon is much good unless it can hit the target, and both the British and American tanks are well-provided with electronic aids. Laser rangefinders take the range to the target in a split second; this is fed to a computer which is programmed with the ballistic performance of the ammunition and gun, and is then modified by sensors which detect the local temperature, cross-wind speed and direction, any tilt of the tank due to rough terrain and several other factors. All these are combined by the computer and a solution is passed to the sight, where it moves the cross-wires of the gunner's telescope. He relays the gun, placing the wires on the target, and fires, and the chances of a first round hit are very high indeed.

Saudi Arabia is equipped with 290 French AMX-30S tanks, another previously relatively untested design. These have a 105mm gun which fires ammunition similar to that fired by the Abrams but, of course, of less weight and therefore less penetrative ability. It also has the ability to fire standard high explosive shells and illuminating shells, which makes

it a very versatile infantry support machine, capable of taking on soft targets such as machine gun posts rather more successfully than the Challenger or Abrams which are, in the last analysis, tank-fighting machines.

The best of the Iraqi tanks was the T72G; this carries a 125mm smoothbore gun firing a fin-stabilised armor-piercing shot similar to that of the Abrams, and it is fitted with an automatic loading mechanism which, in theory, allows 8 shots every minute. In practice, it appears that the reliability of this auto-loader is questionable, and it is likely to

RIGHT: Egyptian troops, with their M60A3 tanks, arrive at Yanbu, a Red Sea port of Saudi Arabia, in September 1990. Egypt has over 800 of these tanks.

LEFT: A British-built Chieftain tank, with 120mm rifled gun, belonging to the Kuwaiti Army, and which managed to escape from Kuwait at the time of the Iraqi invasion.

jam at a critical moment. On the whole the T72, Abrams and Challenger appear to be fairly matched in armament, but the fire control system in the Western tanks will probably show a decisive edge over the less advanced system used in the T72.

The earlier Iraqi tanks, the T54, 55 and 62, have largely been updated in recent years. The T54s have principally been training vehicles and represented little value as battle tanks, but the T55 series had been fitted with the 125mm gun and autoloader of the T72. Some also had additional armor plating installed on the hull and turret to improve the protection. The T62s are an improvement on the original T55, with a 115mm smooth-bore gun. This also has an automatic loading system which is something of a drawback, since the tank turret cannot be moved while the loader is in operation; moreover, ejection of the fired cartridge case is through a hatch in the rear of the turret and, according to reports, the case sometimes misses the hatch and is bounced back inside the turret. Iraq also owned a number of Chinese Type 59 and Type 69-2 main battle tanks, which are something of an unknown quantity in the West. They are basically improvements on the Soviet T-54 series, which China obtained from Russia in the 1950s and then manufactured. The Type 59 is simply the T-54 with a better 100mm smooth-bore gun and im-

RIGHT: An M1A1 Abrams tank of the US 24th Infantry Division maneuvering in the Saudi desert.

LEFT: An ex-Soviet BMP-2 armored infantry fighting vehicle seen in Kuwait City after the Iraqi invasion. Note the elevated 30mm automatic cannon and the double doors at the rear of the 7-man troop compartment.

BELOW: An Iraqi T-62 tank dug into a defensive position and partly concealed by date palms. Note the ammunition and fuel resupply vehicles concealed under the palms while they carry out their replenishment task.

RIGHT: A troop of M2 Bradley IFVs with their rear ramp doors down ready to load troops.

RIGHT: The 3-man crew (commander, gunner and driver) of a 1st Armored Division Bradley make their feelings clear for the camera.

RIGHT: An M3 Bradley of the 1st US Cavalry Division is unloaded from a ship onto a Saudi dockside. The M3 is externally identical to the M2 but has greater ammunition capacity.

BELOW: M2 Bradley infantry fighting vehicles of the US Army during a desert exercise. These have a 25mm gun, TOW missiles, and carry six infantrymen plus a three-man crew.

proved fire control, while the Type 69, of which Iraq may have had as many as 250, is a considerably improved Type 59 with a new 100mm rifled gun, adopted since it was found more accurate than the smoothbore. Both tanks fire Chinese-developed armor-piercing and high explosive projectiles, and the Type 69 also has a modernised electronic fire control system incorporating a laser range-finder and infra-red night sights.

The other side of the coin is the matter of protection, and here again there are several unanswered questions. All three principal tanks use advanced forms of composite armor, using layers of ceramics, steel and titanium, and in some cases with explosive reactive armor (ERA) mounted outside the tank. Composite armor protects by placing layers of very different material for the penetrator to defeat; thus a hard metal penetrator might be blunted by the ceramic layer and turned aside or even shattered by striking a titanium insert. On the other hand an attack by high explosive will be defeated by the varying melting points of the layers, and by chemical interlayering which absorbs the heat of the explosive attack before it can have effect on the metal of the armor. Much of this area is under security wraps and nothing has been published, but, equally, nothing had

ever previously been tried in a real war situation, so the various arguments of the armor engineers and the ammunition engineers remain to be settled.

ERA (explosive reactive armor) consists of thin boxes of high explosive which are fitted to the outside of the tank. In theory, ERA should explode as an attacking projectile touches, and the blast should deflect or destroy the projectile, or the explosive jet from a missile, before it even reaches the main armor. But this is another system which has never been tested in war, and it remains to be seen whether it has done in combat what its designers claimed it would.

ABOVE: Volunteers of the Iraqi People's Army parading in Baghdad in September 1990. The rifles are Romanian versions of the Soviet AKM, with forward hand grips and 40-round magazines.

ABOVE: US troops firing a Dragon anti-armor missile; the soldier nearest the camera is the observer, watching for a fresh target while the launch operator deals with this one.

RIGHT: An air defense squad of the US 82nd Airborne Division. The lead man has a radio on the air defense network, and his companion carries a 'Stinger' missile.

LEFT: Paratroopers of the US 82nd Airborne Division with their 'Hummer' reconnaissance vehicle, returning from a desert patrol.

## ARTILLERY

Conventional artillery is another area in which Iraq was quantitatively superior, with some 3000 towed guns, 500 self-propelled (SP) guns, some 200 field rocket systems and about 50 surface-to-surface missile launchers. However, closer study reveals that much of this artillery was relatively worthless, and the number of modern pieces, capable of reaching ranges comparable with the guns of the Coalition were relatively few.

Their most advanced artillery weapons were the 155mm GHN-45 and G-5 gun-howitzers procured from Austria and South Africa during the war against Iran. Both these weapons fire 100-pound projectiles with stub wings which give added lift and so extend the range, and they can also fire 'base bleed' shells which, burning a pyrotechnic charge as they fly, reduce the base drag and so give even more range. Both the GHN-45 and G-5 can reach to 19 miles with normal shells, 24 miles with base bleed.

Self-propelled artillery in Iraqi hands included a number of US M109 155mm howitzers, plus a far greater number of Soviet 122mm and 152mm pieces. These were the 122mm 2S1 which fires a 48-pound shell to 9.5 miles range, and the 152mm 2S3 firing a 97 pound shell to 11.5 miles. This perform-

ance is not particularly good by modern standards, but it could have been offset by the fact that both weapons were mounted in heavily armored, turreted vehicles which could locate well forward in the battle area. More conventional SP guns, less well armored, or towed guns without any protection would find it difficult to operate so far forward, and this would tend to remove the disadvantage of the lesser range.

Another SP gun the Iraqi army owned is the French 'GCT', a 155mm howitzer of very modern type. This uses an automated loading system, allowing it to be easily operated by only four men, or even by only two men in emergency, and can fire a 97 pound shell to

TOP: The M109A3 155mm self-propelled howitzer 'Bodacious', crew chief Staff Sergeant Tapper of the US Army, being unloaded in a Saudi Arabian port.

ABOVE: Moving an M198 155mm howitzer of the Marine Corps to a new position. Notice the use of sand matting to prevent the vehicle and gun from sinking into patches of soft sand.

RIGHT: An M102 105mm field howitzer of the US Army almost entirely concealed beneath a camouflage net. The 105mm howitzer is organic to the infantry division and has a range of 10 miles with rocket-boosted shells.

BELOW: An M198 155mm howitzer of the US Marine Corps being resupplied with ammunition from the truck in the background. The M198 is air-portable and fires to a range of 14 miles with standard shells.

RIGHT: A launch unit of the Multiple Launch Rocket System (MLRS) fires one of its 227mm rockets. Carrying a 307kg warhead these have a range in excess of 20 miles.

17.5 miles. It is believed that 85 of these guns were in service.

The only Iraqi guns used in the earliest stages were the Soviet-supplied 130mm M46 which fires a 73-pound shell to a range of 17 miles. It is believed that Iraq had ordered a number of M84 conversions of this gun from Yugoslavia; this takes the 130mm gun carriage and mounts a 155mm barrel, giving the resulting weapon performance equal to that of the GHN-45 and G-5, but it is uncertain whether any of these had actually been delivered to Iraq.

US forces relied upon their well-proven M109 SP howitzer. In its most recent M109A3 version this fires a 95-pound projectile to 11 miles range, though with a rocket-boosted shell this range increases to 15 miles. The same weapon was used by the British, who also fielded their 150mm FH-70 towed howitzer, firing a similar shell to 16 miles or a base-bleed shell to 20 miles range.

Both the US and British placed more reliance upon the Multiple Launch Rocket System (MLRS), another new weapon previously untried in war. MLRS consists of a twelve-rocket unit carried on a tracked vehicle which contains its own fire control system. The rockets are loaded in pre-packed pods of six, the vehicle computer is given its own location and that of the target, the firing data is computed and the rockets are automatically fired. Each rocket is 227mm (approx. 10 inches) in diameter and 4m (13 feet) long, and carries a number of sub-munitions. The rocket goes to the target area and there splits open to disperse the sub-munitions over the ground beneath. A salvo of 12 rockets can deposit almost 8000 bomblets

BELOW: An MLRS launcher with the launch module traversed to the side ready to fire. The twelve individual rocket pods can be seen inside the module. The vehicle is an entirely self-contained unit with its own fire control and position-locating system.

RIGHT: A South African G-5 155mm howitzer firing. Numbers of these were supplied to Iraq during the Iraq–Iran war. They fire Extended Range Full Bore (ERFB) shells to a maximum range of 19 miles, or to 24 miles with base bleed.

into an area of about 27 hectares, and each bomblet can defeat the top armor of a tank or burst so as to shower the immediate area with fragments. Other warheads can carry anti-tank mines or anti-tank sub-missiles. The maximum range is said to be in excess of 20 miles, though the exact figure is still secret.

Iraqi rocket launchers were principally adaptations of a Brazilian design, the 'Astros', known as the 'Sajeel' system. The Sajeel 30 is a 32-barrel launcher firing a 127mm rocket to 24 miles, the Sajeel 40 a 180mm rocket to 20 miles and the Sajeel 60 a 300mm rocket to 44 miles. The -40 and -60 versions have sub-munition warheads, though not of the same capacity or effective-ness as those of MLRS. The advantage of these systems is their ability to place large salvos of rockets into an area very rapidly, though the accuracy is not of the same order as that of MLRS.

Iraq also has a number of Soviet FROG (Free Rocket Over Ground) weapons. These

RIGHT: A battery of Iraqi 130mm M-46 guns, supplied by the USSR. These fire a 73-pound shell to a range of 17 miles and were the principal Iraqi guns used during the war.

BELOW: US Marine Lance Corporal Jim Clark, of Ogdensburg, New York, about to fire a 60mm mortar. These light and portable weapons have a range of over 2 miles and form a useful 'pocket artillery' for the Marine infantryman.

are solid-fuel free-flight rockets weighing over one ton and capable of a maximum range of 55 miles. Iraq has developed its own sub-munition warheads for these rockets, as well as chemical agent warheads. One of the tactical advantages of FROG is that it is simple and quick to emplace and fire; unlike the liquid-fuelled Scud missile, it takes very little time to set up the launcher, point it and fire.

The various versions of the Scud missile employed by Iraq are discussed in the air warfare chapter (*see* page 18).

Air defense artillery has been prominent, particularly around Baghdad, though much of it had no more than nuisance value. The hundreds of light 20mm and 30mm weapons

ABOVE: Another element of the US air defense network is this 'Vulcan' 20mm Gatling gun mounted on an M113 armored personnel carrier. It has a rate of fire of 6000 rounds per minute.

RIGHT: Troops of the Iraqi Army parading in Baghdad Stadium, October 1990. They are armed with a locally-manufactured version of the Soviet Kalashnikov AKM rifle.

LEFT: The Brazilian Avibras Astros II SS-30 rocket launcher firing a 127mm rocket. The Iraqi Army call this the 'Sajeel 30' and it has a maximum range of 24 miles.

could only really have been useful against low-flying attacks and could have no effect on stand-off bombing or high-altitude aircraft. These can only be dealt with by the larger calibers, 85mm, 100mm and 130mm. The examples in Iraqi hands were all Soviet weapons and although they have adequate performance – the 130mm can fire a 72-pound shell to a vertical range of 65,000 feet – they are only as good as their fire control systems, and these were fairly elderly. Few Western armies now employ air defense artillery in the major calibers, since they are far less effective than air defense missiles; but, having said that, where guns are employed in numbers, the laws of probability are such that they are bound to have some effect. It is likely that, when the final analysis is made, whatever success the Iraqi air defenses may have had against Allied aircraft will prove to have been due to missiles rather than guns.

## CHEMICAL WARFARE

The threat of chemical warfare is more real now than it has been since World War One, and the armory of chemical agents at Iraq's disposition was formidable. Mustard, phosgene and nerve agents have certainly been manufactured in Iraq and some were used in the Iran war and also against the Kurdish uprising in Iraq itself. Nevertheless, the threat of chemical attack is generally worse

well. But the effectiveness of chemical attack relies upon swamping the target with gas so that it can take effect rapidly and before the occupants of the target area can take precautions. This argues a large concentration of artillery, so as to deliver the necessary number of shells rapidly on to the same point, and this, in turn, is the weakness of the system, since large concentrations of artillery can easily be detected by satellites and other surveillance systems and be attacked before they are ready to begin their task.

Missiles and rockets, such as Scud, FROG and the Sajeel systems were a greater threat than artillery since each projectile carries a far greater payload; FROG, for example, carries a 1000-pound warhead and that of Scud is heavier. Either of these, filled with nerve agent and burst in the air over a target, could cover a considerable area with a lethal con-

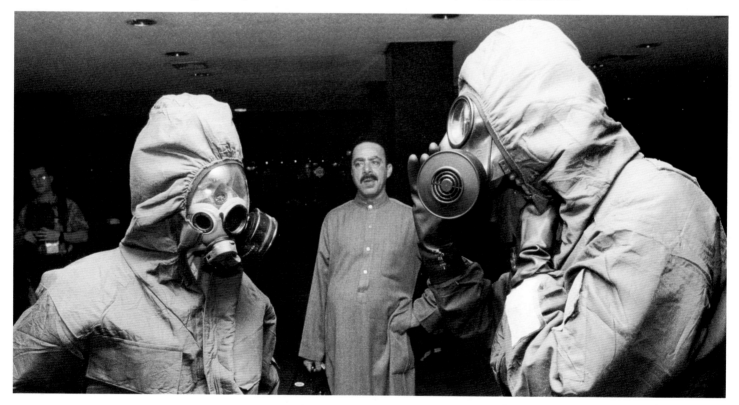

than the reality; so far as mustard and phosgene, the two deadliest conventional gases, are concerned, records show that only about 2 percent of trained troops attacked by these gases actually die, the remainder recovering after a period of some weeks. Nerve gases are another question, since they are systemic poisons which most certainly will kill if inhaled or if splashed on the exposed skin, so the danger from these is far greater.

Delivery of these agents can be performed in a number of ways, and so far as ground weapons is concerned the most obvious method is by artillery or by rockets. It is known that Iraq had stocks of chemically-charged shells in 130mm caliber and there were probably stocks in 155mm caliber as

centration. Equally, the multiple Sajeel launcher could have been able to saturate an area with 32 rockets at one shot, though these would have smaller warheads.

The threat of chemicals is countered by the wearing of masks and protective suits, and in this lies the advantage of the weapon; not to cause casualties, but simply to disable the threatened troops by encumbering them. The demand to wear a heavy, impervious, overall suit and a mask in temperatures reaching three figures is a certain way of sapping the mobility and agility of troops and slowing down their reaction times. If for no other reason, the neutralisation of Iraqi chemical warfare weapons came high on the list of Allied priorities.

ABOVE: American (left) and British (right) soldiers compare their anti-gas equipment in front of a Saudi hotel during a chemical alert drill.

ABOVE: Syrian Special Forces troops during an anti-gas drill, wearing Soviet-made gasmasks.

RIGHT: Two soldiers of the 164th Armored Battalion, US 24th Infantry Division, assist each other into their anti-gas equipment during an alert.

# SHIPS and NAVAL WEAPONS

## THE IRAQI NAVY

Even if the Iraqi Navy's planned expansion had occurred it would still have been a small force by international standards. The long reliance on the Soviet Union for armaments was reflected in the two Osa I and five Osa II missile-armed fast attack craft which formed the core of the fleet. The 38.6m craft were armed with SS-N-2 Styx anti-ship missiles (SS-N-2B in the later boats) and two twin 30mm gun mounts, and were driven by three-shaft diesels at a top speed of 34 knots. Two Osa I and three Osa II boats were sunk by the Iranians during the previous conflict.

In 1980 the 1850-ton frigate *Ibn Khaldum* (renamed *Ibn Marjid*) was delivered by a Yugoslav shipyard, to provide training for crews of new ships to be built by Italy. She was armed with a Bofors 57mm dual-purpose gun, a 40mm L/70 gun and eight 20mm guns, but is reported to have had four MM-38 or MM-40 Exocet anti-ship missiles added amidships subsequently.

Early in 1981 orders were placed with Italian shipyards to supply four 2500-ton frigates of the *Lupo* type and six 680-ton missile corvettes similar to the *Wadi* class built earlier for Libya. The *Lupo* class ships are similar to their sisters in the Italian, Peruvian and Venezuelan navies, with a 127mm L/54 gun forward, eight Otomat Mk 2 anti-ship missiles, two twin 40mm L/70 gun mountings and an Aspide short-range air defense missile system. Propulsion is two-shaft gas turbine and diesel, developing a maximum speed of 35 knots. The missile corvettes form two groups, one group of two equipped with a flight deck and hangar for an Augusta A-109A light helicopter. The armament is six Otomat Mk 2 missiles (two in the helicopter-equipped pair), an Aspide SAM system, a 76mm gun and a twin 40mm L/70 gun mount, and triple torpedo-launchers. They are driven by four-shaft diesels at a maximum speed of 37.5 knots.

All ten ships were completed, along with a replenishment tanker, the *Agnadeen* (similar to the Italian Navy's *Stromboli* class), in 1984-87 but the Italian Government would not permit delivery while the war between Iraq and Iran continued. The ceasefire resulted in the lifting of the embargo in the spring of 1989, but the only ship of the group to leave Italian waters was the *Agnadeen*, which reached Alexandria in 1986, where she remains. The Iranian Government announced that it would treat any Iraqi ships transiting the Straits of Hormuz as hostile,

PREVIOUS PAGE: The USS *Wisconsin* (BB-64) firing her 16-inch guns. She and her sister *Missouri* also launched cruise missiles in Desert Storm.

BELOW: The missile frigate USS *Reid* FFG-30) in company with a British supply ship in the Gulf.

RIGHT: A Polnocny-D landing ship, similar to the Iraqi ships sunk off the coast of Kuwait.

RIGHT: The Iraqi missile corvettes *Mussa ben Hussain* and *Tariq Ibn Ziad* lying in La Spezia awaiting settlement of the outstanding payments to the shipbuilders.

LEFT: Admiral William M. Fogarty, USN, Commander of the Middle East Joint Task Force briefing the press aboard the flagship USS *La Salle* (AGF-3).

and subsequent disputes over payments resulted in all deliveries being frozen. Late in 1990 the builders Fincantieri formally asked the Italian Government for permission to seek foreign buyers for the ships, which were obviously costing them a substantial and growing amount of money to maintain at La Spezia and Alexandria.

Amphibious warfare ships included three Soviet-supplied Polnocny-D type 1150-ton tank landing craft delivered in 1977-79 (a fourth was sunk by Iranian missiles in 1981). In 1983 a Danish shipyard delivered three 5800-ton modified roll-on/roll-off cargo vessels, the *Al Zahraa* class.

## WAR LOSSES

It is difficult to identify individual warships from the somewhat terse communiques issued by the Coalition forces between the start of hostilities on 16 January and the ceasefire on 27 February. At least 13 Iraqi warships were sunk or disabled by three Royal Navy Lynx helicopters firing Sea Skua anti-ship missiles. These include a Polnocny-D landing craft and the Yugoslav-built salvage ship *Aka*, both sunk, and two ex-Kuwaiti TNC 45 missile boats, also sunk. Other hits claimed include an assault craft, two ex-Soviet minesweepers, three more ex-

LEFT: The Royal Navy destroyer HMS *York* (left) and the frigate *Jupiter* (background) were in the Gulf when Iraq invaded Kuwait.

RIGHT: A Royal Navy Lynx HAS.2 helicopter, equipped with Yellow Veil ALQ-167 jammer pod, IR flare decoy launchers and Orange Crop ESM gear.

ABOVE: The USS *La Salle* is a former amphibious assault ship converted to serve as a command ship for the Middle East.

LEFT: The air defense destroyer USS *Scott* was originally ordered for the Shah of Iran's navy and served as part of the *Eisenhower*'s group in Desert Shield.

Kuwaiti missile boats and two ex-Soviet Zhuk type patrol craft. The RN ships operating the Lynx helicopters were the air defense destroyers *Cardiff*, *Gloucester* and *Manchester* and the frigate *Brazen*.

On 21 January US Navy A-6 aircraft from the carrier USS *Ranger* disabled what was described as a mercantile-type minelayer, leaving her to be sunk later by Saudi forces. Three days later another A-6 aircraft destroyed an Iraqi minesweeper off Qurah Island, some 45 miles SE of Kuwait City; a second minesweeper apparently struck an Iraqi mine and sank while trying to escape. An SH-60B SeaHawk helicopter from the frigate USS *Nicholas* (FFG-47) came under fire from the Iraqi garrison on the island while trying to rescue survivors. On the same day US aircraft sank another patrol boat, a tanker was bombed and a hovercraft was sunk (believed to be one of six SRN.6 types bought in 1981). Navy aircraft sank at least one Osa boat and are reported to have damaged a frigate, presumably the *Ibn Marjid*. The Iraqi Navy was virtually wiped out by the end of January, after only two weeks.

**Nominal Strength of the Iraqi Navy on 16 January 1991**

| No. | Type | Name/Class | Subsequent fate |
| --- | --- | --- | --- |
| 1 | frigate | *Ibn Marjid* | Damaged, possibly sunk |
| 3 | LCTs | *Atika* | 1 sunk |
| 3 | LSTs | *Al Zahraa* | |
| 7 | FACs | *Nisan* | several damaged, possibly sunk |
| 4(?) | FACs ex-Kuwaiti | TNC 45 | at least 2 sunk |
| 2(?) | FACs ex-Kuwaiti | FPB 57 | |
| 3 | patrol craft | SO 1 type | |
| 6 | MTBs | P 6 type | |
| 2 | patrol craft | Poluchat 1 type | |
| 5 | patrol craft | Zhuk type | 2 sunk |
| 1 | patrol craft | Nyryat II type | |
| 2 | patrol craft | PO 2 type | |
| 2 | patrol craft | Bogomol type | |
| 9 | patrol craft | PB 90 type | |
| 3 | m/sweepers | Yevgenya type | |
| 2 | m/sweepers | Nestin type | |
| 2 | m/sweepers | T 43 type | both sunk |

BELOW: HMS *York* escorting a large tanker in the Gulf during the build-up to Desert Storm.

## IRAQI MISSILE SYSTEMS

The major naval weapons in Iraqi hands at the beginning of the crisis were an estimated 400 AM-39 Exocet anti-ship missiles, possibly 80-100 SS-N-2 or SS-N-2B Styx missiles and an undisclosed number of Chinese FL-1 Silkworm coast defense missiles (Western designation CSS-N-2). The Exocet earned notoriety in the Falklands War in 1982, and hit a number of tankers during the Tanker War between Iraq and Iran in the mid-1980s; it also disabled the frigate USS *Stark* in 1987.

Only one Exocet attack was made during the recent conflict, but the F1-EQ5 Mirage was shot down by one of the carrier group's combat air patrol (CAP). In the last week of fighting a Silkworm was fired at the battleship *Missouri*'s battle group, but it was destroyed by a Sea Dart fired by HMS *Gloucester*.

The air-launched AM-39 Exocet has a range of 50-70km (27-38 nautical miles, whereas the ship-launched version has a range of 42km (23 nm). The MM-40 version, which equipped the Kuwaiti FPB 57 and TNC 45 type missile boats has a slightly longer range, 65km (35nm).

## UNITED STATES' FORCES

The dominant naval partner in the coalition against Saddam Hussein was the United States Navy, which immediately despatched the nuclear carrier *Dwight D Eisenhower* from the Mediterranean to the Gulf, with her battle group, in August 1990. Within days of the invasion of Kuwait the carrier *Saratoga* and the battleship *Wisconsin* and their respective groups were leaving Stateside ports en route for the Gulf. They were joined by the *John F Kennedy, Ranger, America, Theodore Roosevelt* and *Midway* battle groups by

the end of December, but the inevitable need to relieve the carriers in rotation meant that by the end of December there were six carrier battle groups on station, and an additional battleship, the USS *Missouri*. An additional carrier, the *Forrestal* was relieved in the Eastern Mediterranean by the British support carrier HMS *Ark Royal* to enable her to provide reinforcements if needed.

The *Midway* (CV-41) is the oldest USN carrier, having been completed in 1945. She has undergone many modernisations but was due to decommission at the end of 1991. The *Forrestal* (CV-59) is expected to be relegated to training duties by the end of the year, but

BELOW: The battleship *Wisconsin* lies at anchor in the Gulf.

LEFT: The nuclear-powered aircraft carrier USS *Dwight D Eisenhower* (CVN-69) in the Mediterranean before the Kuwait Crisis.

BELOW: The battleship *Wisconsin* was one of the first heavy naval units to enter the Gulf in September 1990.

her sisters *Saratoga* (CV-60), *Ranger* (CV-61) and *Independence* (CV-62) will serve into the next century. The *America* (CV-66) is one of three similar *Kitty Hawk* class, displacing 81,800 tons fully loaded and driven by four-shaft steam turbines at a speed of 33 knots. The *John F Kennedy* (CV-67) is an improved version, and the last oil-fuelled carrier built for the USN. The other carriers in the Gulf operations were members of the *Nimitz* (CVN-68) class, displacing over 83,000 tons and driven by nuclear reactors at a maximum speed of 33 knots. The *Dwight D Eisenhower* (CVN-69) completed her scheduled four-month overhaul a month early, and she sailed in mid-February for a post-overhaul shakedown. The *Theodore Roosevelt* (CVN-71) is the first of a new class of improved *Nimitz* type.

USN carrier air groups vary from wing to wing and are assigned to carriers in rotation, so it is not easy to identify exactly which aircraft serve on board each carrier. A typical air group comprises 24 F-14A Tomcat fighters, 24 F/A-18 fighter/attack aircraft, 10 A-6E Intruder attack aircraft, 4 KA-6D tankers, 4 EA-6B Prowler electronic warfare aircraft, 4 E-2C Hawkeye airborne early warning aircraft, 10 S-3A Viking anti-submarine aircraft and 6 SH-3H Sea King ASW helicopters. By the end of January roughly one-third of the 15,000 air sorties of Desert

Storm had been made by carrier aircraft, flown by USN and USMC pilots.

Each carrier battle group is provided with a heavy escort against surface, air and submarine threats. These include *Ticonderoga* (CG-47) class Aegis cruisers, older missile cruisers of the *Belknap* (CG-26), *Leahy* (CG-16), *Virginia* (CGN-38) and *California* (CGN-36) classes, *Spruance* (DD-963), *Kidd* (DDG-993), *Charles F Adams* (DDG-2) and *Coontz* (DDG-38) class destroyers, and *Knox* (FF-1052) and *Oliver Hazard Perry* (FFG-7) class frigates.

ABOVE: The primary mission of the Aegis cruiser *Ticonderoga* (CG-47) is to escort carrier battle groups.

ABOVE: The destroyer USS *John Rodgers* (DD-983) is armed with armored box launchers for Tomahawk cruise missiles.

In addition to the wide variety of air-launched weapons, ranging from the new AGM-84E Standoff Land Attack Missile (SLAM) to terminally guided weapons such as the Maverick anti-tank missile and laser-guided bombs, these ships are defended by Standard SM-1 and SM-2 missiles in medium-range (MR) and extended-range (ER) versions, with interception ranges of 35-180,000 metres in their various forms.

Fleet fighters form the outer layer of air defense, followed by the second layer of area defense missiles, and individual ships are armed with Sea Sparrow missiles for point or self-defense. As a last-ditch defense against anti-ship missiles leaking through these layers the ships are equipped with Mk 15 Phalanx 20mm close-in weapon systems (CIWS). Each Phalanx fires a 'wall of lead' (actually depleted uranium or tungsten shot)

RIGHT: The US Marine Corps operates Air Cushion Landing Craft (LCACs) for high-speed amphibious assault. This example is seen on land in Saudi Arabia.

from its six barrels, to destroy the missile.

USN warships are also armed with offensive weapons, notably the RGM-84 Harpoon anti-ship missile and various types of Tomahawk cruise missiles. The 75-80nm Harpoon is carried in quadruple groups of canisters on deck or in conventional and vertical missile magazines. The 300nm Tomahawk is mounted in armored box launchers on deck or in vertical launch magazines. The first strike against Iraqi land targets involved 52 Tomahawks and about 200 in all were launched. The missile is used primarily to destroy airfields and fortified positions but it also exists in a strategic version, with a nuclear warhead. By the end of November the build-up of Tomahawk strength was evident; the Aegis cruiser *San Jacinto* (CG-56) had been rearmed with no fewer than 122 Tomahawks in her two vertical launch magazines, and her sisters *Antietam* (CG-54) and *Philli-pine Sea* (CG-58) were also reported to be carrying an increased load of Tomahawks. At least 350 Tomahawks were available by the beginning of December.

LEFT: A seaman aboard the frigate USS *Jack Williams* (FFG-24) aims a Stinger missile during a Silkworm missile alert.

BELOW: The cruiser USS *England* (CG-22) in the Gulf with the British frigate HMS *Battleaxe* in the background.

RIGHT: The two battleships' 16-inch guns fired HE, HC and SADARM shells during Desert Storm.

LEFT: The Aegis cruiser USS *Vincennes* (CG-49) achieved notoriety by shooting down an Iranian airliner during the previous Gulf conflict.

RIGHT: The *Vincennes* also served with the Desert Shield forces and is armed with Standard SM-2 (MR) SAMs, Harpoon SSMs and Tomahawk SLCMs.

Unique to the US Navy are the four *Iowa* class 57,000 ton battleships, built in the Second World War but modernised in the 1980s to serve as missile- and gun-platforms, retaining their nine 16-inch guns but receiving 16 Harpoon missiles and 32 Tomahawks and four Mk 15 Phalanx CIWS. The *Missouri* (BB-63) and *Wisconsin* (BB-64) launched cruise missiles in the early stages of the campaign and pounded shore positions with their guns towards the end. Each 16-inch Mk 7 gun fires a 2700-pound shell a maximum of 40,000 metres, at the rate of two rounds per minute. The armor-piercing (AP) round can penetrate 30 feet of concrete, while the high-capacity (HC) round creates craters 50 feet wide and 20 feet deep. For the first time the two battleships also fired new SADARM type shells, each spreading 666 bomblets or sub-munitions over 45,000 square meters. Four-shaft geared steam turbines drive the battleships at over 30 knots and at half-speed they have an endurance of 15,000 miles.

In support of the surface warships and the carriers the US Marine Corps also deployed the 26th Marine Expeditionary Unit (the *Inchon* Group), the 4th Marine Expeditionary Brigade (the *Nassau* Group) and the 13th

LEFT: The destroyer USS *Tattnall* (DDG-19) transiting the Suez Canal in August 1990.

RIGHT: Radar plotters in the operations room of the British frigate HMS *Battleaxe*.

BELOW LEFT: The 36,000 ton fleet oiler USS *Neosho* (T-AO-143) carries 180,000 barrels of fuel oil.

BELOW: The frigate USS *Brewton* (FF-1086) was one of the escorts with the aircraft carrier *Independence*'s battle group.

BOTTOM: The fleet oiler *Cimarron* (AO-177) also served with the *Independence* and can replenish two conventionally-powered carriers and up to eight escorts.

Marine Expeditionary Unit (the *Okinawa* Group). The most powerful amphibious ships in the world are the *Tarawa* (LHA-1) class amphibious assault ships, 39,300 ton ships capable of lifting nearly 2000 marines and their vehicles as well as support aircraft and helicopters. The *Iwo Jima* (LPH-2) class amphibious assault helicopter carriers were the first ships built from the keel up to operate assault helicopters, and they can lift over 2000 marines.

The more traditional amphibious ships are the *Whidbey Island* (LSD-41), *Austin* (LPD-4), *Raleigh* (LPD-1) and *Anchorage* (LSD-36) classes of dock landing ships and amphibious transport docks, descendants of the dock landing ships developed in the Second World War, and the *Newport* class tank landing ships (LSTs). In all the amphibious forces included one LHA, four LPHs, ten LSDs and LPDs, seven LSTs and an amphibious transport (LKA).

Clearly the USN had no intention of being caught in a mine trap, as it had been in 1987, when obsolescent Iranian mines (Russian design but supplied by North Korea) blocked the channel leading to Kuwait City. The mine countermeasures group was carried to the Gulf aboard the heavy-lift ship *Super Servant 3:* the new *Avenger* (MCM-1) and three elderly ocean minesweepers of the *Acme* and *Aggressive* classes. These ships are equipped

to hunt for mines using a high-definition sonar and a remotely operated disposal vehicle. However, they were unable to prevent the Aegis cruiser *Princeton* (CG-59) and the assault ship *Tripoli* (LPH-10) from being damaged. In all 25 contact mines were found floating in the Northern Gulf, and all were blown up by USN ordnance disposal divers. The traditional method of sinking by rifle fire could not be used in case the mine sank to the bottom in shallow water, where it could remain dangerous.

The USN also uses large helicopters for mine clearance, CH-53E Super Stallions and MH-53E Sea Dragons to tow a variety of sensors and sleds carrying noisemakers and magnetic coils. This method was used to clear the Suez Canal in 1984 and again in the Gulf in 1987-88 but no news has so far been released of similar operations in the Gulf this time.

## OTHER NAVIES

The second biggest contingent was provided by the Royal Navy, which provided *Birmingham* and *Manchester* class air defense destroyers and *Broadsword, Boxer* and *Leander* class frigates, as well as five 'Hunt' Class mine countermeasures vessels (MCMVs). The destroyers are armed with the GWS.30 Sea Dart area defense missile, capable of a range of 40,000 metres (about 25 miles), while the frigates have the GWS.25 Sea Wolf anti-missile system, and MM-38 Exocet anti-ship missiles. Both classes are equipped with HAS.2 Lynx helicopters, armed with Sea Skua anti-ship missiles. Sea Skua was de-

signed to deal with missile boats and corvettes, and has a range of 15km. It was used successfully for the first time in the Falklands conflict and proved a brilliant success in the recent fighting.

The Royal Fleet Auxiliary helicopter training ship *Argus* was sent out to act as a hospital ship but her Sea King Commando HC.4 helicopters were also used to move the massive array of stores and equipment needed by the ground forces. Four other RFA ships were also in the area, the repair ship *Diligence*, the supply ship *Fort Grange*, and the oilers *Olna* and *Orangeleaf*.

RN minehunters had cleared mines in the Gulf in 1987-88, but in August 1990 three 'Hunt' Class were sent (later increased to five), and HMS *Herald* was hurriedly converted to serve as a support ship. She was later relieved by her sister *Hecla*, which supported the *Atherstone, Cattistock, Dulver-*

ABOVE: Loading a Sea Wolf missile launcher aboard HMS *Battleaxe* during Desert Shield.

RIGHT: The destroyer HMS *Cardiff* is armed with GWS.30 Sea Dart SAMs, a 4.5inch Mk 8 gun and two Mk 15 Phalanx CIWS Gatlings.

LEFT: Typical of many Gulf navies' fast attack craft, the Qatari *Damsah* is armed with MM-40 Exocet missiles.

RIGHT: Royal Navy ships in the Gulf were supported by supply ships such as RFA *Orangeleaf*.

BELOW: The Spanish frigate *Numancia* is similar to the US Navy's *Oliver Hazard Perry* (FFG-7) class.

ton, *Ledbury* and *Hurworth*. These 'Hunt' Class ships are equipped with a Type 193M hull-mounted sonar, as well as magnetic, acoustic and wire sweeps, and two PAP-104 remotely operated vehicles.

Three Canadian warships were given a hurried update to improve their defenses against missile attack. The destroyer escort *Terra Nova* and the destroyer *Athabaskan* were re-armed with Mk 15 Phalanx CIWS and the *Terra Nova* was also given Harpoon missiles, while the oiler *Protecteur* was given a twin 3-inch 50 cal. gun mount and two Phalanx CIWS, and the CH-124 Sea King helicopters embarked in the three ships exchanged their ASW equipment for Kestrel ESM and other electronic warfare equipment. A squadron of CF-18 Hornet fighters was also sent Qatar to provide air cover for the squadron.

On 13 August the Royal Australian Navy sent the frigates *Adelaide* and *Darwin* to the Gulf, followed by the replenishment ship *Success*. The frigates are virtually identical to the US Navy's *Oliver Hazard Perry* (FFG-7) class, 3000 ton ships armed with Standard SM-1 (MR) and Harpoon missiles, and equipped with one S-70B2 SeaHawk and one Squirrel helicopter each. The air defense destroyer *Brisbane* and the frigate *Sydney* were earmarked as reliefs. The *Brisbane* is similar to the US Navy's *Charles F Adams* class

DDGs, and is armed with Standard SM-1 (MR), Harpoon and Ikara missiles, while the *Sydney* is a sister of the *Adelaide* and *Darwin*. Before sailing the *Brisbane* was hurriedly fitted with two Phalanx CIWS.

The Federal German Navy send five MCM ships to the Eastern Mediterranean, an example followed by Belgium. Denmark sent the corvette *Olfert Fischer,* Spain sent the frigates *Santa Maria, Descubierta* and *Cazadora* (later relieved by other escorts), Norway sent the coast guard ship *Andenes,* and Argentina sent the destroyer *Almirante Brown* and the corvette *Spiro*. The Italians built up their forces to three frigates and a support ship in the Straits of Hormuz and kept four minehunters in the Red Sea. The Royal Netherlands Navy replaced its ships in mid-November, sending the air defense frigate HrMS *Jacob van Heemskerck,* the ASW frigate *Philips van Almonde* and the supply ship *Zuiderkruis*. Reflecting growing concern about Iraq's large stock of Exocet missiles, the *Zuiderkruis* was given a Goalkeeper 30mm CIWS to bring her to the same standard as the two frigates. Greece sent a frigate as did Portugal, and even Poland sent a hospital ship, the *Wodnik,* while New Zealand offered its new support ship *Endeavour* to operate with the Australian ships.

The French Navy sent the carrier *Clemenceau,* but her normal air group was replaced by 40 helicopters. Machinery troubles reduced the carrier's speed to 28 knots and her steam catapult was out of action, and she was later forced to return to Toulon. To neutralise

LEFT: The Australian destroyer HMS *Brisbane* (DDG-41) was hurriedly rearmed with two Mk 15 Phalanx CIWS for the Gulf (the starboard one is clearly visible).

BOTTOM LEFT: The French carrier *Clemenceau* could only operate helicopters because her steam catapult was faulty. She later returned to Toulon with engine trouble.

BELOW: The Netherlands air defense frigates *Witte de With* and *Jacob van Heemskerck* are armed with Standard SM-1 (MR) and Harpoon missiles.

LEFT: A BMARC 20mm gun aboard a Royal Navy warship in the Gulf.

BELOW: Loading a Mk 15 Phalanx CIWS aboard the British air defense destroyer HMS *York*.

any threat to Turkey, NATO's Naval On-Call Force in the Mediterranean (NAVOCFORMED) remained together after its annual exercise in October. Another fear was that Libya might make some unilateral gesture, either firing Scud missiles or laying mines to sink chartered ships carrying military cargoes to the Gulf. Nothing came of this threat, but it occupied the minds of the coalition's naval planners.

## CONCLUSION

The reliability, even more than the accuracy of modern air-flight weapons came as a surprise to most people. The first Tomahawk strike scored a 98 percent success, something which could not have been achieved ten years ago. The dense air defense over the ships operating anywhere near Iraqi air-

fields or shore defenses made it impossible for any Iraqi aircraft to launch effective attacks, and in any case the Iraqi Air Force chose to absent itself from the contest. However, the lack of hostile air activity did mean that various types of warships fulfilled the roles for which they were designed. The two battleships provided awesome firepower, all as part of General Schwarzkopf's deception plan.

Although the campaign did not involve an amphibious assault the large force of US Marines afloat played a vital role in deceiving the Iraqi commanders about the direction of the land assault. Marine detachments fought well on land and their AV-8B Harrier II STOVL aircraft and helicopter gunships provided close support in the land battle and the preliminary softening up of Iraqi defenses.

Sea power's contribution to the victorious outcome of Desert Storm can best be summed up by simple statistics. Aircraft flew in roughly 95 percent of the personnel required for Desert Shield and Desert Storm, but official sources confirm that about 95 percent of the equipment, stores, fuel, ammunition, food and spares went to Saudi Arabia by sea. By mid-February the United States Government alone was using 223 merchant ships, either chartered or called up from reserve. Had Saddam Hussein's forces been able to cut that supply-line they would have.

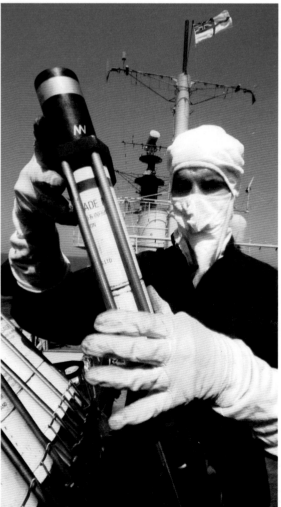

ABOVE: The Sea Skua helicopter-launched anti-ship missile has also been developed in a surface-to-surface version.

LEFT: Loading a Barricade decoy launcher aboard the frigate HMS *Jupiter* in the Gulf.

RIGHT: Warshot Sea Dart area defense missiles on the launcher aboard HMS *York*, with the 4.5inch Mk 8 gun in the background.

BELOW: The French PAP-104 remotely operated mine disposal vehicle was used by many coalition MCM craft to hunt for Iraqi mines.

ABOVE: An M1 Abrams on the move in the Saudi desert.

ACKNOWLEDGMENTS

The authors and publishers would like to thank Design 23 who designed this book and the following agencies and individuals for the supply of illustrations on the pages noted.

Aviation Photographs International: 15 top.
Bell Publishing Group Pty: 76 top.
British Aerospace: 25 top, 78 top.
Tony Bryan/Peter Sarson: 22-23, 34-35.
Crown Copyright, Ministry of Defence UK: 4 top & bottom, 14 below, 22 center, 24, 31, 32 both, 60, 62 top, 63 top, 64, 65, 68-69, 73 top, 74 lower, 75 top & bottom, 77 top & right, 78 lower, 79 top.
Société ECA: 79 lower.
French Navy: 76 bottom.
Grumman: 17 lower.
Avions Marcel Dassault: 22 top.
Richard Natkiel: 9.
*via* Naval Forces: 61 center.
Royal Netherlands Navy: 77 bottom left.
Reuters/Bettmann: 2-3, 4 center, 7 all three, 8 top, 10 both, 11 both, 12-13, 20 both, 25 lower, 26, 27 both, 38, 39 top, 42 both, 43 lower, 44, 45 all three, 46 center & below, 47, 48 top, 54 left & top, 55 lower, 56-57 all three, 61 bottom, 68 top, 70, 72 top.
John See: 28-29.
Sikorsky Helicopters: 33 top.
H.M. Steele: 61 top, 75 center.
Thomson CSF: 74 top.
TRH Pictures: 53, 54 right.
United States' Dept of Defense: 1. 14 top, 15 below, 17 top, 18 both, 19, 21 below, 28, 30-31, 33 lower, 35 lower, 36-37, 39 lower, 40 top, 43 top, 46 top, 48 lower, 49 both, 50-51 all four, 52, 52-53, 55 top, 58-59, 62 lower, 63 lower, 66-67 all five, 71 both, 72 below, 73 lower two.